W9-BNI-763

THE WORDS OF GANDHI

ALSO IN THE "WORDS OF" SERIES

The Words of Peace: Selections from the Speeches of the Winners of the Nobel Peace Prize
Selected and Edited by
Irwin Abrams

The Words of Martin Luther King, Jr.
Selected and Introduced by
Coretta Scott King

The Words of Albert Schweitzer
Selected and Introduced by
Norman Cousins

The Words of Harry S Truman
Selected and Introduced by
Robert J. Donovan

The Words of Desmond Tutu
Selected and Introduced by
Naomi Tutu

THE WORDS OF GANDHI

SELECTED AND INTRODUCED BY
RICHARD ATTENBOROUGH

Afterword by Johanna McGeary

wm
WILLIAM MORROW
An Imprint of HarperCollins*Publishers*

The "Words Of" Series

HarperCollins books may be purchased for educational, business, or sales promotional use. For information please write: Special Markets Department, HarperCollins Publishers, 10 East 53rd Street, New York, NY 10022.

Words of Mohandas K. Gandhi are reprinted with the kind permission of the Navajivan Trust, Bombay, India.
Photographs of Mohandas K. Gandhi courtesy of the National Gandhi Museum, New Delhi, India.
Photograph on page 115 by Frank Connor taken during the filming of *Gandhi* © 1982 by Indo-British Films Ltd.
The publisher wishes to acknowledge the support and cooperation of Columbia Pictures in the publication of this book.

First published by Newmarket Press in 1982.

FIRST WILLIAM MORROW PAPERBACK EDITION PUBLISHED 2012.

Library of Congress Cataloging-in-Publication Data
Gandhi, Mahatma, 1869–1948
[Selections. 2000]
The words of Gandhi / selected and with an introduction by Richard Attenborough.
p. cm. — (The Newmarket "Words Of" series)
Includes bibliographical references.
1. Gandhi, Mahatma, 1869–1948—Philosophy.
2. Gandhi, Mahatma, 1869–1948—Quotations.
I. Attenborough, Richard. II Title. III. Series.

DS481.G3A25 2000
954.03'5—dc21 00-038700

ISBN 978-1-55704-468-6 (paperback)

ISBN 978-1-55704-807-3 (hardcover)

12 13 14 15 16 RRD 10 9 8 7 6 5 4 3 2 1

CONTENTS

Introduction by Richard Attenborough *vii*

DAILY LIFE 1

COOPERATION 17

NONVIOLENCE 33

FAITH 61

PEACE 73

Notes *93*

Glossary *96*

Afterword by Johanna McGeary *97*

Chronology *108*

Bibliography *113*

Gandhi as barrister, Johannesburg, South Africa.

Gandhi as satyagrahi at the beginning of his civil disobedience campaign in South Africa.

INTRODUCTION

In 1962 Mortilal Kothari, a London-based Indian civil servant, asked me to make a film on the life of the Mahatma. I had only a rudimentary schoolboy's knowledge of Gandhi as the leader of the Indian people's struggle for independence from Britain. I therefore agreed to read a biography and some of his own writings.

At the age of twenty-three, in 1893, shortly after he had arrived in South Africa as an attorney to conduct a case for an Indian trading company, he wrote one sentence which knocked me off my feet. "It has always been a mystery to me how men can feel themselves honoured by the humiliation of their fellow beings." He had just witnessed Indians forced to walk in the gutter so that whites could pass unimpeded along the sidewalk.

His words struck me so forcibly that there and then I committed myself to an attempt to make a film about Mahatma Gandhi—a commitment that changed the subsequent twenty years of my life. Since then, every career decision I have made has been tempered by my love affair with this one project.

Gandhi had its world premiere in New Delhi on 30 November 1982.

Mohandas K. Gandhi was born in 1869 to Hindu parents in the state of Gujerat in western India. He entered an arranged marriage with Kasturbai Makanji when both were thirteen years old. His family later sent him to London to study law, and in 1891 he was admitted to the Inner Temple, and called to the bar. In Southern Africa he worked ceaselessly to improve the rights of immigrant Indians. It was there that he developed his creed of passive resistance against injustice, *satyagraha,* meaning "truth force," and was frequently jailed as a result of the protests that he led. Before he returned to India with his wife and children in 1915, he had radically changed the lives of Indians living in Southern Africa.

Back in India, it was not long before he was taking the lead in the long struggle for independence from Britain. He never wavered in his unshakable belief in nonviolent protest and religious tolerance. When his Muslim and Hindu compatriots committed acts of violence, whether against the British who ruled India, or against each other, he fasted until the fighting ceased. Independence, when it came in 1947, was not a military victory, but a triumph of human will. To Gandhi's despair, however, the country was partitioned into Hindu India and Muslim Pakistan. The last months of his life were spent trying to end the appalling violence which ensued, leading him to fast to the brink of death, an act which finally quelled the riots. In January 1948, at the age of seventy-nine, he was killed by the bullets of a Hindu assassin as he walked through a crowded garden in New Delhi to take evening prayers.

I hope this book, *The Words of Gandhi,* will offer an introduction to the Mahatma's ideas and philosophies.

Albert Einstein was moved to say of Gandhi: "Generations to come will scarce believe that such a one as this ever in flesh and blood walked upon this earth."

—Richard Attenborough

The words of Gandhi that follow have been selected from writings published over a span of four decades and represent only a small part of his voluminous work.

In discussing the value of his words, Gandhi stressed the importance of action:

"I have nothing new to teach the world. Truth and nonviolence are as old as the hills. All I have done is to try experiments in both on as vast a scale as I could. In doing so, I have sometimes erred and learnt by my errors. Life and its problems have thus become to me so many experiments in the practice of truth and nonviolence . . .

"Well, all my philosophy, if it may be called by that pretentious name, is contained in what I have said. But, you will not call it 'Gandhism'; there is no 'ism' about it. And no elaborate literature or propaganda is needed about it. The scriptures have been quoted against my position, but I have held faster than ever to my position that truth may not be sacrificed for anything whatsoever. Those who believe in the simple truths I have laid down can propagate them only by living them."

"I have not the shadow of a doubt that any man or woman can achieve what I have, if he or she would make the same effort and cultivate the same hope and faith."

DAILY LIFE

"Strength does not come from physical capacity. It comes from an indomitable will."

"It is because we have at the present moment everybody claiming the right of conscience without going through any discipline whatsoever that there is so much untruth being delivered to a bewildered world."

"I have learnt through bitter experience the one supreme lesson: to conserve my anger, and as heat conserved is transmuted into energy, even so our anger controlled can be transmuted into a power which can move the world."

"Joy lies in the fight, in the attempt, in the suffering involved, not in the victory itself."

"Man must choose either of the two courses, the upward or the downward; but as he has the brute in him, he will more easily choose the downward course than the upward, especially when the downward course is presented to him in a beautiful garb. Man easily capitulates when sin is presented in the garb of virtue."

"Life is greater than all art. I would go even further and declare that the man whose life comes nearest to perfection is the greatest artist; for what is art without the sure foundation and framework of a noble life?"

"Literacy must be one of the many means for intellectual development, but we have had in the past intellectual giants who were unlettered."

"Literacy is not the end of education, or even the beginning."

"Literary education should follow the education of the hand—the one gift that visibly distinguishes man from the beast. It is a superstition to think that the fullest development of man is impossible without a knowledge of the art of reading and writing. That knowledge undoubtedly adds grace to life, but is in no way indispensable for man's moral, physical or material growth."

"To forget how to dig the earth and tend the soil is to forget ourselves."

"The music of life is in danger of being lost in the music of the voice."

"Don't be dazzled by the splendour that comes to you from the West. Do not be thrown off your feet by this passing show. The Enlightened One has told you in never-to-be-forgotten words that this little span of life is but a passing shadow, a fleeting thing, and if you realize the nothingness of all that appears before your eyes, the nothingness of this material case that we see before us ever changing, then indeed there are treasures for you up above, and there is peace for you down here, peace which passeth all understanding, and happiness to which we are utter strangers. It requires an amazing faith, a divine faith and surrender of all that we see before us."

"In India we have three million people who have to be satisfied with one meal a day, and that meal consists of a *chapati* containing no fat in it and a pinch of salt. You and I have no right to anything we have until these three millions are clothed and fed better. You and I, who ought to know better, must adjust our wants, and even undergo voluntary starvation in order that they may be nursed, fed and clothed."

"God alone is the judge of true greatness because He knows men's hearts."

"The distinguishing characteristic of modern civilization is an indefinite multiplicity of human wants. The characteristic of ancient civilization is an imperative restriction upon and a strict regulating of these wants."

"If I preach against the modern artificial life of sensual enjoyment, and ask men and women to go back to the simple life epitomized in the *charkha*, I do so because I know that without an intelligent return to simplicity, there is no escape from our descent to a state lower than brutality."

"The golden rule . . . is resolutely to refuse to have what millions cannot. This ability to refuse will not descend upon us all of a sudden. The first thing is to cultivate the mental attitude that will not have possessions or facilities denied to millions, and the next immediate thing is to rearrange our lives as fast as possible in accordance with that mentality."

"This is the unmistakable teaching of the Gita. He who gives up action falls. He who gives up only the reward rises. But renunciation of fruit in no way means indifference to the result. In regard to every action one must know the result that is expected to follow, the means thereto, and the capacity for it. He, who, being thus equipped, is without desire for the result, and is yet wholly engrossed in the due fulfillment of the task before him, is said to have renounced the fruits of his action."

"Just as one must not receive, so must one not possess anything which one does not really need. It would be a breach of this principle to possess unnecessary foodstuffs, clothing or furniture. For instance, one must not keep a chair if one can do without it. In observing this principle one is led to a progressive simplification of one's own life."

"Love is the subtlest force in the world."

"One man cannot do right in one department of life whilst he is occupied in doing wrong in any other department. Life is one indivisible whole."

"All of your scholarship, all your study of Shakespeare and Wordsworth would be vain if at the same time you did not build your character and attain mastery over your thoughts and your actions."

"Purity of life is the highest and truest art."

"Even if, without fulfilling the whole law of sacrifice, that is, the law of our being, we perform physical labour enough for our daily bread, we should go a long way towards the ideal. If we did so, our wants would be minimized, our food would be simple. We should then eat to live, not live to eat. Let anyone who doubts the accuracy of this proposition try to sweat for his bread; he will derive the greatest relish from the productions of his labour, improve his faith and discover that many things he took were superfluities."

"Individual liberty and interdependence are both essential for life in society."

"It is beneath human dignity to lose one's individuality and become a mere cog in the machine."

"The only tyrant I accept in this world is the 'still small voice' within."

"All is well with you even though everything seems to go dead wrong, if you are square with yourself. Reversely, all is not well with you although everything outwardly may seem to go right, if you are not square with yourself."

"Does not the history of the world show that there would have been no romance in life if there had been no risks?"

"The goal ever recedes from us. The greater the progress the greater the recognition of our unworthiness. Satisfaction lies in the effort, not in the attainment. Full effort is full victory."

"True knowledge gives a moral standing and moral strength."

"To call women the weaker sex is a libel; it is man's injustice to women."

"The wife is not the husband's bondslave, but his companion and his help-mate and an equal partner in all his joys and sorrows—as free as the husband to choose her own path."

"You will guard your wife's honour and be not her master, but her true friend. You will hold her body and her soul as sacred as I trust she will hold your body and your soul. To that end you will have to live a life of prayerful toil, and simplicity and self-restraint. Let not either of you regard another as the object of his or her lust."

"We notice (love) between father and son, between brother and sister, friend and friend. But we have to learn to use that force among all that lives, and in the use of it consists our knowledge of God. Where there is love there is life; hatred leads to destruction."

"Love is a rare herb that makes a friend even of a sworn enemy and this herb grows out of nonviolence."

"The law of love could be best understood and learned through little children."

"I hold myself to be incapable of hating any being on earth. By a long course of prayerful discipline, I have ceased for over forty years to hate anybody. I know this is a big claim. Nevertheless, I make it in all humility."

"Absolute calm is not the law of the ocean. And it is the same with the ocean of life."

"It does not require money to be neat, clean and dignified."

"Chastity is not a hothouse growth."

"Chastity is one of the greatest disciplines without which the mind cannot attain requisite firmness."

"I do not believe . . . that an individual may gain spirituality while those who surround him suffer. I believe in *advaita,** I believe in the essential unity of man and for that matter, of all that lives. Therefore, I believe that if one man gains spirituality, the whole world gains with him and if one man falls the whole world falls to that extent."

**advaita*: One of the two principal branches of Vedanta, which is one of the six classical systems of Indian philosophy. It holds that Brahman, the Self, is ultimate reality, and that the world has come into being from Brahman and is wholly dependent on it.

"To a true artist only that face is beautiful which, quite apart from its exterior, shines with the truth within the soul."

"Birth and death are not two different states, but they are different aspects of the same state."

"Learning takes us through many stages in life but it fails us utterly in the hours of dangers and temptation."

"Whenever you are in doubt or when the self becomes too much with you, try the following expedient: Recall the face of the poorest and most helpless man you have ever seen and ask yourself if the step you contemplate is going to be of any use to him. Will he be able to gain anything by it? Will it restore to him control over his own life and destiny? In other words, will it lead to . . . self-rule for the hungry and spiritually starved millions of our countrymen? Then you will find your doubts and your self melting away."

COOPERATION

"Democracy, disciplined and enlightened, is the finest thing in the world."

"My notion of democracy is that under it the weakest should have the same opportunity as the strongest."

"The spirit of democracy cannot be established in the midst of terrorism, whether governmental or popular."

"In my humble opinion, non-cooperation with evil is as much a duty as is cooperation with good."

"The spirit of democracy is not a mechanical thing to be adjusted by abolition of forms. It requires change of the heart."

"Little do town dwellers know how the semi-starved masses of India are slowly sinking to lifelessness. Little do they know that their miserable comfort represents the brokerage they get for the work they do for the foreign exploiter, that the profits and the brokerage are sucked from the masses. Little do they realize that the Government established by law in British India is carried on for this exploitation of the masses. No sophistry, no jugglery in figures, can explain away the evidence that the skeletons in many villages present to the naked eye."

"The economics that disregard moral and sentimental considerations are like wax works that being life-like still lack the life of the living flesh. At every crucial moment these newfangled economic laws have broken down in practice. And nations or individuals who accept them as guiding maxims must perish."

"Machinery to be well used has to help and ease human effort. The present use of machinery tends more and more to concentrate wealth in the hands of a few in total disregard of millions of men and women whose bread is snatched by it out of their mouths."

"I claim for the *charkha* the honour of being able to solve the problem of economic distress in a most natural, simple, inexpensive and business-like manner. The *charkha*, therefore, is not only not useless . . . but is a useful and indispensable article for every home. It is the symbol of a nation's prosperity and, therefore, freedom. It is a symbol not of commercial war but of commercial peace."

"The spinning wheel means national consciousness and a contribution by every individual to a definite constructive national work."

"It was our love of foreign cloth that ousted the wheel from its position of dignity."

"If India was to escape such a disaster, it had to imitate what was best in America and other western countries and leave aside its attractive-looking but destructive economic policies. Therefore, real planning consisted in the best utilization of the whole manpower of India and the distribution of the raw products of India in her numerous villages instead of sending them outside and re-buying finished articles at fabulous prices."

"A true and nonviolent combination of labour would act like a magnet attracting to it all the needed capital. Capitalists would then exist only as trustees. When that happy day dawned, there would be no difference between capital and labour. Those who labour will have ample food, good and sanitary dwellings, all the necessary education for their children, ample leisure for self-education and proper medical assistance."

"As I look at Russia where the apotheosis of industrialization has been reached, the life there does not appeal to me. To use the language of the Bible, 'What shall it avail a man if he gain the whole world and lose his soul?' In modern terms, it is beneath human dignity to lose one's individuality and become a mere cog in the machine. I want every individual to become a full-blooded, fully developed member of society."

"The introduction of manual training will serve a double purpose in a poor country like ours. It will pay for the education of our children and teach them an occupation on which they can fall back in later life, if they choose, for earning a living. Such a system must make our children self-reliant. Nothing will demoralize the nation so much as that we should learn to despise labour."

"A nation that is capable of limitless sacrifice is capable of rising to limitless heights. The purer the sacrifice the quicker the progress."

"My patriotism is not an exclusive thing. It is all-embracing and I should reject that patriotism which sought to mount upon the distress of the exploitation of other nationalities. The conception of my patriotism is nothing if it is not always, in every case, without exception, consistent with the broadest good of humanity at large."

"Just as the cult of patriotism teaches us today that the individual has to die for the family, the family has to die for the village, the village for the district, the district for the province, and the province for the country, so a country has to be free in order that it may die, if necessary, for the benefit of the world."

"Political power means capacity to regulate national life through national representatives. If national life becomes so perfect as to become self-regulated, representation becomes unnecessary. There is then a state of enlightened anarchy. In such a state everyone is his own ruler. He rules himself in such a manner that he is never a hindrance to his neighbor. In the ideal state, therefore, there is no political power because there is no state. But the ideal is never fully realized in life. Hence the classical statement of Thoreau that the government is best which governs least."

"Let us not push the mandate* theory to ridiculous extremes and become slave to resolutions of majorities. That would be a revival of brute force in a more virulent form. If rights of minorities are to be respected, the majority must tolerate and respect their opinion and action . . . It will be the duty of the majority to see to it that the minorities receive a proper hearing and are not otherwise exposed to insults."

"Government of the people by the people and for the people cannot be conducted at the bidding of one man, however great he may be."

"Liberty never meant the license to do anything at will."

---

*mandate: An authorization given by an electorate to its representatives to act in a specific way on an issue.

"There is no human institution without its dangers. The greater the institution the greater the chances of abuses. Democracy is a great institution and therefore it is liable to be greatly abused. The remedy, therefore, is not avoidance of democracy but reduction of possibility of abuse to a minimum.

"The Congress* has become a vast democratic body. It reached a high water-mark during the past twelve months. Without being technically on the register millions took possession of it and added lustre to it. But goondaism† also entered the Congress to a much larger extent than hitherto. It was inevitable. The ordinary rules prescribed for the selection of volunteers were practically set aside during the last stages of the struggle. The result has been that in some places goondaism has made itself felt. Some Congressmen have been threatened with disaster if they will not give the money demanded of them. Of course, professional goondas may also take advantage of the atmosphere and ply their trade.

"The wonder is that the cases I have in mind are so very few compared to what they might have

---

*Congress: Indian National Congress, political party founded in 1885, long the dominant political force in India.

†goonda: Rogue or hoodlum.

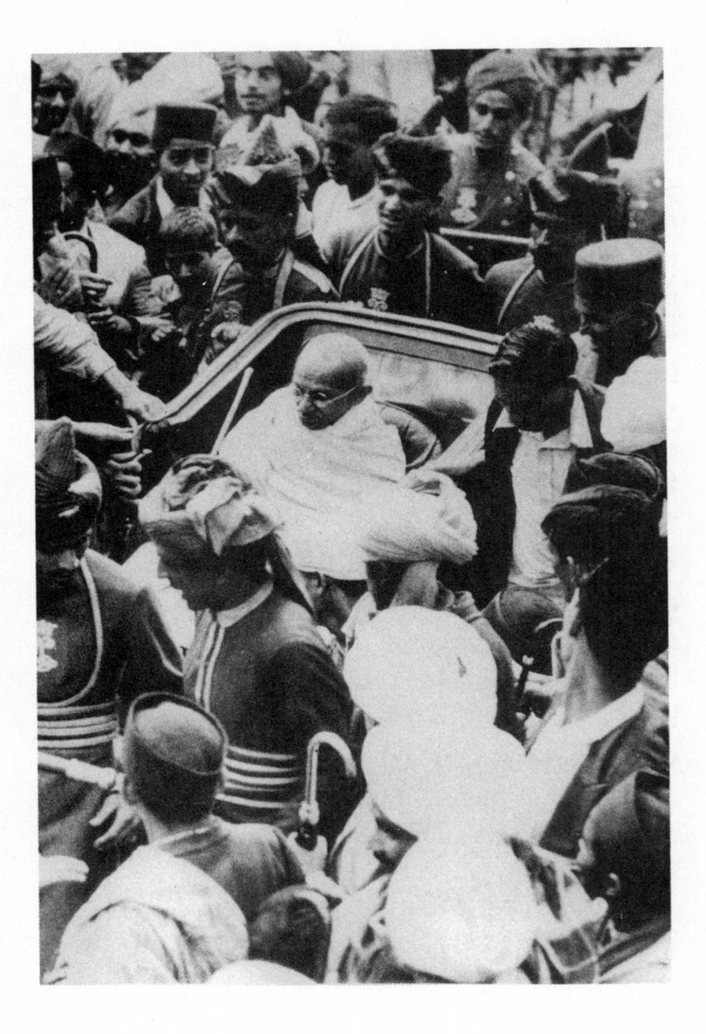

been, regard being had to the great mass awakening. My conviction is that this happy state is due to the Congress creed of nonviolence, even though we have but crudely followed it. But there has been sufficient expression of goondaism to warn us to take time by the forelock and adopt preventive and precautionary measures."

"In mass civil resistance leadership is essential; in individual civil resistance every resister is his own leader."

"Good travels at a snail's pace. Those who want to do good are not selfish, they are not in a hurry, they know that to impregnate people with good requires a long time."

NONVIOLENCE

"Nonviolence and cowardice go ill together. I can imagine a fully armed man to be at heart a coward. Possession of arms implies an element of fear, if not cowardice. But true nonviolence is an impossibility without the possession of unadulterated fearlessness."

"Nonviolence should never be used as a shield for cowardice. It is a weapon for the brave."

"I see neither bravery nor sacrifice in destroying life or property for offence or defence."

"It is no nonviolence if we merely love those that love us. It is nonviolence only when we love those that hate us. I know how difficult it is to follow this grand law of love. But are not all great and good things difficult to do? Love of the hater is the most difficult of all. But by the grace of God even this most difficult thing becomes easy to accomplish if we want to do it."

"It is the acid test of nonviolence that in a nonviolent conflict there is no rancor left behind and, in the end, the enemies are converted into friends. That was my experience in South Africa with General Smuts.* He started with being my bitterest opponent and critic. Today he is my warmest friend . . ."

"This is in essence the principle of nonviolent non-cooperation. It follows therefore that it must have its root in love. Its object should not be to punish the opponent or to inflict injury upon him. Even while non-cooperating with him, we must make him feel that in us he has a friend and we should try to reach his heart by rendering him humanitarian service whenever possible."

"That is the beauty of *satyagraha*. It comes up to oneself; one has not to go out in search for it."

---

*Smuts, Jan Christian, 1870–1950: South African Boer General. Gandhi's principal adversary during his time in South Africa.

'Truth {*satya*} implies love, and Firmness {*agraha*} engenders and therefore serves as a synonym for force. I thus began to call the Indian movement '*satyagraha*'; that is to say, the force which is born of truth and love or nonviolence . . ."

"*Ahimsa* is the attribute of the soul, and, therefore, to be practiced by everybody in all the affairs of life. If it cannot be practiced in all departments, it has no practical value."

"*Ahimsa* is not the crude thing it has been made to appear. Not to hurt any living thing is no doubt a part of *ahimsa*. But it is its least expression. The principle of *ahimsa* is hurt by every evil thought, by undue haste, by lying, by hatred, by wishing ill to anybody. It is also violated by our holding on to what the world needs."

"*Ahimsa* and Truth are so intertwined that it is practically impossible to disentangle and separate them. They are like two sides of a coin, or rather a smooth unstamped metallic disc. Who can say which is the obverse and which the reverse? Nevertheless, *ahimsa* is the means; Truth is the end."

"In this age of the rule of brute force, it is almost impossible for anyone to believe that anyone else could possibly reject the law of the final supremacy of brute force. And so I receive anonymous letters advising me that I must not interfere with the progress of non-cooperation even though popular violence may break out. Others come to me and, assuming that secretly I must be plotting violence, inquire when the happy moment for declaring open violence will arrive. They assure me that the English will never yield to anything but violence, secret or open. Yet others, I am informed, believe that I am the most rascally person living in India because I never give out my real intention and that they have not a shadow of a doubt that I believe in violence just as much as most people do.

"Such being the hold that the doctrine of the sword has on the majority of mankind, and as success of non-cooperation depends principally on absence of violence during its pendancy, and as my views in this matter affect the conduct of a large number of people, I am anxious to state them as clearly as possible.

"I do believe that where there is only a choice between cowardice and violence I would advise violence. Thus when my eldest son asked me what he should have done, had he been present when I was almost fatally assaulted in 1908, whether he should have run away and seen me killed or

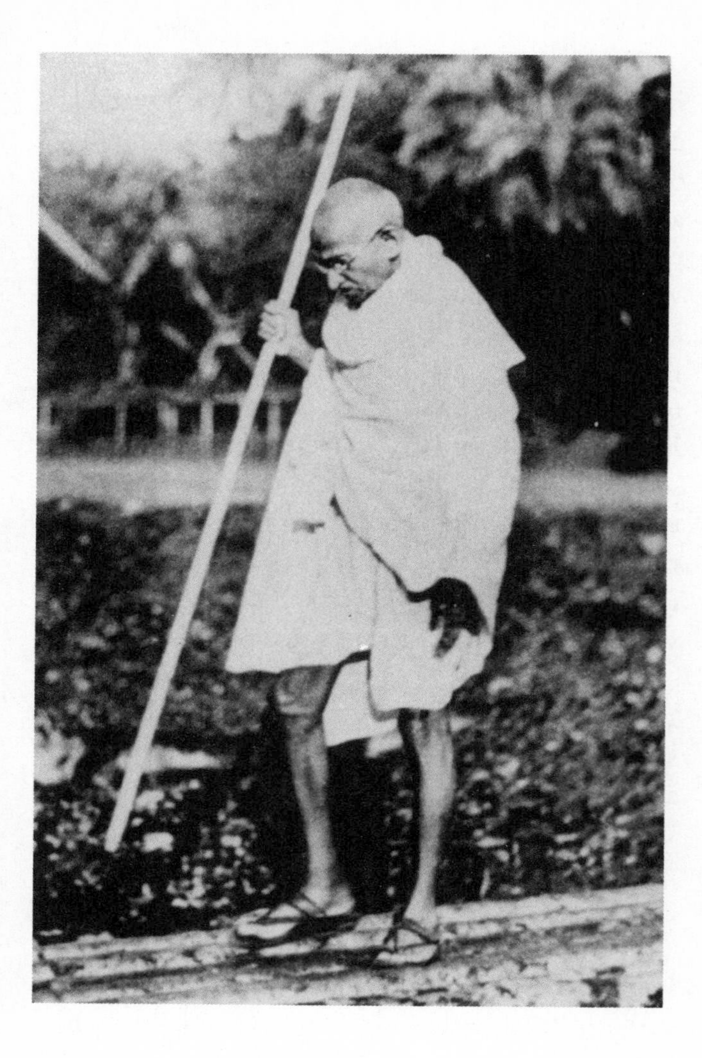

whether he should have used his physical force which he could and wanted to use, and defended me, I told him that it was his duty to defend me even by using violence. Hence it was that I took part in the Boer War, the so-called Zulu rebellion and the late War.* Hence also do I advocate training in arms for those who believe in the method of violence. I would rather have India resort to arms in order to defend her honour than that she should in a cowardly manner become or remain a helpless witness to her own dishonour.

"But I believe that nonviolence is infinitely superior to violence, forgiveness is more manly than punishment. 'Forgiveness adorns a soldier.' But abstinence is forgiveness only when there is the power to punish; it is meaningless when it pretends to proceed from a helpless creature. A mouse hardly forgives a cat when it allows itself to be torn to pieces by her. I, therefore, appreciate the sentiment of those who cry out for the condign punishment of General Dyer† and his ilk. They would tear him to

---

*Boer War: War in South Africa, 1899–1902, in which Great Britain defeated the settlers of Dutch ancestry (Boers).

Zulu rebellion: Clash in 1904 in the South African province of Natal between Zulu tribesmen and the white government. Gandhi led an ambulance corps for the British.

†Dyer, Brigadier General Reginald E.: British officer responsible for the massacre of Indian civilians in Amritsar, 1919.

pieces if they could. But I do not believe myself to be a helpless creature. Only I want to use India's and my strength for a better purpose.

"Let me not be misunderstood. Strength does not come from physical capacity. It comes from an indomitable will. An average Zulu is any day more than a match for an average Englishman in bodily capacity. But he flees from an English boy, because he fears the boy's revolver or those who will use it for him. He fears death and loses his nerve in spite of his burly figure. We in India may in a moment realize that one hundred thousand Englishmen need not frighten three hundred million human beings. A definite forgiveness would therefore mean a definite recognition of our strength. With enlightened forgiveness must come a mighty wave of strength in us, which would make it impossible for a Dyer and a Frank Johnson to heap affront upon India's devoted head. It matters little to me that for the moment I do not drive my point home. We feel too downtrodden not to be angry and revengeful. But I must not refrain from saying that India can gain more by waiving the right of punishment. We have better work to do, a better mission to deliver to the world.

"I am not a visionary. I claim to be a practical idealist. The religion of nonviolence is not meant merely for the *rishis* and saints. It is meant for the common people as well. Nonviolence is the law of our species as violence is the law of the brute. The spirit lies dormant in the brute and he knows no law but that of physical might. The dignity of man requires obedience to a higher law—to the strength of the spirit.

"I have therefore ventured to place before India the ancient law of self-sacrifice. For *satyagraha* and its offshoots, non-cooperation and civil resistance, are nothing but new names for the law of suffering. The *rishis* who discovered the law of nonviolence in the midst of violence were greater geniuses than Newton. They were themselves greater warriors than Wellington. Although knowledgeable in the use of arms, they realized their uselessness and taught a weary world that its salvation lay not through violence but through nonviolence.

"Nonviolence in its dynamic condition means conscious suffering. It does not mean meek submission to the will of the evildoer, but it means the pitting of one's whole soul against the will of the tyrant. Working under this law of our being, it is possible for a single individual to defy the whole might of an unjust empire to save his honour, his religion, his soul, and lay the foundation for that empire's fall or its regeneration.

"And so I am not pleading for India to practise nonviolence because she is weak. I want her to practise nonviolence being conscious of her strength and power. No training in arms is required for realization of her strength. We seem to need it because we seem to think that we are but a lump of flesh. I want India to recognize that she has a soul that cannot perish and that can rise triumphant above every physical weakness and defy the physical combination of a whole world. What is the meaning of *Rama*, a mere human being, with his host of monkeys, pitting himself against the insolent strength of ten-headed *Ravana* surrounded in supposed safety by the raging waters on all sides of *Lanka*?* Does it not mean the conquest of physical might by spiritual strength? However, being a practical man, I do not wait till India recognizes the practicability of the spiritual life in the political world. India considers herself to be powerless and paralysed before the machine guns, the tanks and the airplanes of the English. And she takes up non-cooperation out of her weakness. It must still

---

*Rama: Any of the three avatars (incarnations) of the Hindu god Vishnu: Balarama, Parashurama, or Ramachandra.

Ravana: In the Hindu epic *Ramayana,* the King of Sri Lanka who abducts Sita, the wife of Ramachandra, and is later defeated by him.

serve the same purpose, namely, bring her delivery from the crushing weight of British injustice if a sufficient number of people practise it.

"I isolate this non-cooperation from Sinn Feinism,* for it is so conceived as to be incapable of being offered side by side with violence. But I invite even the school of violence to give this peaceful non-cooperation a trial. It will not fail through its inherent weakness. It may fail because of poverty of response. Then will be the time for real danger. The high souled men, who are unable to suffer national humiliation any longer, will want to vent their wrath. They will take to violence. So far as I know, they must perish without delivering themselves or their country from the wrong. If India takes up the doctrine of the sword, she may gain momentary victory. Then India will cease to be the pride of my heart. I am wedded to India because I owe my all to her. I believe absolutely that she has a mission for the world. She is not to copy Europe blindly. India's acceptance of the doctrine of the sword will be the hour of my trial. I hope I shall not be found wanting. My religion has no geographical limits. If I have a living faith in it, it will transcend my love for India herself. My life is dedicated to

---

*Sinn Feinism: Irish nationalist organization, founded in 1905, advocating complete political separation from Britain.

service of India through the religion of nonviolence which I believe to be the root of Hinduism.

"Meanwhile I urge those who distrust me, not to disturb the even working of the struggle that has just commenced, by inciting to violence in the belief that I want violence. I detest secrecy as a sin. Let them give nonviolent non-cooperation a trial and they will find that I had no mental reservation whatsoever."

"The force of nonviolence is infinitely more wonderful and subtle than the material forces of nature, like electricity."

"The force generated by nonviolence is infinitely greater than the force of all the arms invented by man's ingenuity."

"Although non-cooperation is one of the main weapons in the armory of *satyagraha,* it should not be forgotten that it is, after all, only a means to secure the cooperation of the opponent consistently with trust and justice . . .

Avoidance of all relationships with the opposing power, therefore, can never be a *satyagrahi*'s object, but transformation or purification of that relationship."

"Strength of numbers is the delight of the timid. The valiant in spirit glory in fighting alone."

"Disobedience to be civil has to be open and nonviolent."

"Disobedience, to be civil, implies discipline, thought, care, attention."

"Civil disobedience is the inherent right of a citizen. He dare not give it up without ceasing to be a man. Civil disobedience is never followed by anarchy. Criminal disobedience can lead to it. Every state puts down criminal disobedience by force. It perishes, if it does not. But to put down civil disobedience is to attempt to imprison conscience."

"Nonviolence succeeds only when we have a real living faith in God."

"I do not believe in short-violent-cuts to success . . . However much I may sympathize with and admire worthy motives, I am an uncompromising opponent of violent methods even to serve the noblest of causes . . . Experience convinces me that permanent good can never be the outcome of untruth and violence."

"Nonviolence implies voluntary submission to the penalty for non-cooperation with evil."

"We must (then) evolve order out of chaos. And I have no doubt that the best and speediest method is to introduce the people's law instead of mob law.

"One great stumbling block is that we have neglected music. Music means rhythm, order. Its effect is electrical. It immediately soothes. I have seen, in European countries, a resourceful superintendent of police by starting a popular song control the mischievous tendencies of mobs. Unfortunately, like our Shastras,* music has been the prerogative of the few, either the barter of prostitutes or high-class religious devotees. It has never become nationalized in the modern sense. If I had any influence with volunteer boy scouts and {other} organizations, I would make compulsory a proper singing in company of national songs. And to that end I should have great musicians attending every Congress or Conference and teaching mass music.

"Much greater discipline, method and knowledge must be exacted from volunteers and no chance comer should be accepted as a full-fledged volunteer. He only hinders rather than helps. Imagine the consequences of one untrained soldier finding his way into an army at war. He can disorganize it in a second. My great anxiety about non-cooperation is not the slow response of the leaders, certainly not the well-meant and ill-meant criticism, never unadulterated repression. The movement will overcome these obstacles. It will even gain strength from them. But the greatest obstacle is that we have not yet emerged from the *mobocratic* stage. But my consolation lies in the fact that nothing is so easy as to train mobs, for the simple reason that they have no mind, no premeditation. They act in a frenzy. They repent quickly. Our

---

*Shastras: The sacred books of Hinduism.

organized government does not repent of its fiendish crimes at Jallianwala, Lahore, Kasur, Akalgarh, Ram Nagar, etc.* But I have drawn tears from repentant mobs at Gujranwala† and everywhere a frank acknowledgment of repentance from those who formed the mob during that eventful month of April. Non-cooperation I am therefore now using in order to evolve democracy. And I respectfully invite all the doubting leaders to help by refusing to condemn, in anticipation of a process of national purification, training and sacrifice.

"{Next week} I hope to give some illustrations of how in a moment order was evolved out of mob disorder. My faith in the people is boundless. Theirs is an amazingly responsive nature. Let not the leaders distrust them. This chorus of condemnation of non-cooperation when properly analysed means nothing less than distrust of the people's ability to control themselves. For the present I conclude this

---

*Jallianwala Bagh: Public square in the city of Amritsar, site of the 1919 massacre of Indian civilians by British troops under General Dyer. Lahore: Capital city of Punjab. In a famous case in 1931, three young men were executed here by the British on the basis of very flimsy evidence of wrongdoing. Today Lahore is in Pakistan.

†Gujranwala: City presently located in northeast Pakistan.

somewhat lengthy article by suggesting some rules for guidance and immediate execution.

"1. There should be no raw volunteers accepted for big demonstrations. Therefore none but the most experienced should be at the head.

"2. Volunteers should have a general instruction book on their persons.

"3. At the time of demonstrations there must be a review of volunteers at which special instructions should be given.

"4. At stations, volunteers should not all be centered at one point, namely, where the reception committee should be. But they should be posted at different points in the crowd.

"5. Large crowds should never enter the station. They cannot but inconvenience traffic. There is as much honour in staying out as in entering the station.

"6. The first duty of the volunteers should be to see that other passengers' luggage is not trampled upon.

"7. Demonstrators ought not to enter the station long before the notified time for arrival.

"8. There should be a clear passage left in front of the train for the passengers.

"9. There should be another passage if possible half way through the demonstrators for the heroes to pass.

"10. There should be no chain formed. It is humiliating.

"11. The demonstrators must not move till the heroes have reached their coach or till they receive a prearranged signal from an authorized volunteer.

"12. National cries must be fixed and must be raised not anyhow, at any time or all the time, but just on the arrival of the train, on the heroes reaching the coach and on the route at fair intervals. No objections need be raised to this on the score of the demonstration becoming mechanical and not spontaneous. The spontaneity will depend on numbers, the response to the cries above all the general look of the demonstrators, not in the greatest number of noises or the loudest. It is the training that a nation receives which characterizes the nature of its demonstrations. A Mohammedan silently worshipping in his mosque is no less demonstrative than a Hindu temple-goer making a noise either through his voice or his gong or both.

"13. On the route the crowd must line and not follow the carriages. If pedestrians form part of the moving procession, they must noiselessly and in an orderly manner take their places and not at their own will join or abstain.

"14. A crowd should never press towards the heroes but should move away from them.

"15. Those on the last line or the circumference should never press forward but should give way when pressure is directed towards them.

"16. If there are women in the crowd they should be specially protected.

"17. Little children should never be brought out in the midst of crowds.

"18. At meetings volunteers should be dispersed among the crowd. They should learn flag and whistle signaling in order to pass instructions from one to another when it is impossible for the voice to carry.

"19. It is not up to the audience to preserve order. They do so by keeping motionless and silent.

"20. Above all, everyone should obey volunteers' instructions without question.

"This list does not pretend to be exhaustive. It is merely illustrative and designed to stimulate thought and discussion."

(When Gandhi arrived at Durban from Bombay on 13 January 1897, he was besieged and assaulted by an excited crowd. But Gandhi was rescued by the resourcefulness of a police superintendent. Among the devices he employed for saving Gandhi's life was singing the very tune that the mob was repeating against Gandhi.)

"The measures that suggest themselves to me are naturally and certainly a scientific and more intelligent and disciplined application of nonviolence. In the first place if we had a firmer faith in nonviolence, than we have shown, not one man or woman who did not strictly conform to the rules regarding the admission of volunteers would have been taken. It would be no answer to say that in that case there would have been no volunteers during the final stage and therefore there would have been a perfect failure. My experience teaches me to the contrary. It is possible to fight a nonviolent battle even with one satyagrahi. But it, i.e., a nonviolent battle, cannot be fought with a million nonsatyagrahis. And I would welcome even an utter failure with nonviolence unimpaired rather than depart from it by a hair's breadth to achieve a doubtful success. Without adopting a noncompromising attitude so far as nonviolence is concerned, I can see nothing but disaster in the end. For, at the critical moment we may be found wanting, weighed in the scales of nonviolence, and may be found hopelessly unprepared to meet the forces of disorder that might suddenly be arrayed against us.

"But having made the mistake of indiscriminate recruiting how are we to repair the mischief in a nonviolent way? Nonviolence means courage of the highest order and therefore readiness to suffer. There should therefore be no yielding to bullying, bluff or worse, even though it may mean the loss of a few precious lives. Writers of threatening letters should be made to realise that their threats will not be listened to. But at the same time their disease must be diagnosed and properly treated. Even the goondas are part of us and therefore they must be handled gently and sympathetically. People generally do not take to goondaism for the love of it. It is a symptom of a deeper-seated disease in the body politic. The same law should govern our relations with internal goondaism in the system of government. And if we have felt that we have ability to deal with that highly organised goondaism in a nonviolent manner how much more should we feel the ability to deal with internal goondaism by the same method?

"It follows that we may not seek police assistance to deal with the disease although it is open during the truce to any Congressman to seek it precisely in the same manner as any other citizen. The way I have suggested is the way of reform, conversion, love. Seeking police assistance is the way of punishment, fear, want of affection if not actual disaffection. The two methods therefore cannot run together. The way of reform appears at some stage or other to be difficult but it is in reality the easiest."

"When a man submits to another through fear, he does not follow his nature but yields to brute force. He who has no desire to dominate others by brute force will not himself submit to such force either. Recognizing, therefore, that man who fears brute force has not attained self-knowledge at all, our *Shastras* allowed him the use of brute force while he remains in this state.

"Forgiveness is the virtue of the brave. He alone who is strong enough to avenge a wrong knows how to love (and forgive). He alone who is capable of enjoying pleasures can qualify to be a *brahmachary* by restraining his desires. There is no question of the mouse forgiving the cat. It will be evidence of India's soul-force only if she refuses to fight when she has the strength to do so.

"It is necessary to understand what the phrase 'strength to fight' means in this context. It does not mean only physical strength. Everyone who has courage in him can have the strength to fight, and everyone who has given up fear of death has such strength. I have seen sturdy Negroes cowering before white boys, because they were afraid of the white man's revolver. I have also seen weaklings hold out against robust persons. Thus, the day India gives up fear we shall be able to say that she has the strength to fight. It is not at all true to say that, to be able to fight, it is essential to acquire the ability to use arms; the moment, therefore, a man wakes up to the power of the soul, that very moment he comes to know the strength he has for fighting. That is why I believe that he is the true warrior who does not die killing but who has mastered the *mantra* of living by dying.

"The sages who discovered the never-failing law of nonviolence were themselves great warriors. When they discovered the ignoble nature of armed strength and realized the true nature of man, they discerned the law of nonviolence pervading this world all full of violence. They then taught us that the *atman* can conquer the whole world, that the greatest danger to the *atman* comes from itself and that conquest over it brings us the strength to conquer the entire world.

"But they did not think, nor have they affirmed or taught anywhere, that because they had discovered that law they alone could live according to it. On the contrary, they declared that even for a child the law is the same, and that it can act upon it too. It is not true that only *sannyasis* abide by it; all of us do so more or less, and a law which can be followed partially can be followed perfectly.

"I have been striving to live according to this law. For many years past, I have been consciously trying to do so and have been exhorting India to do the same.

"I believe myself to be an idealist and also a practical man. I do not think that a man can be said to have lived in accordance with this law only if he does so consciously and purposefully. Therefore, like a *vaid* {his medicine}, I place it before all, whether or not they have faith in it. To prove that it is not necessary to have the higher knowledge to be able to recognize the importance of this law, I have joined hands with those who hold views contrary to mine. My friend Shaukat Ali seems to attach prime importance to violence, to believe that it is man's *dharma* to kill his enemy. Consequently, he follows the law of nonviolence with hatred in his heart. He thinks non-cooperation is a weapon of the weak, and therefore, inferior to resistance by force. Even so, he has joined me because he has seen that except non-cooperation, there is no other effective method of upholding the honour of his faith.

"I appeal even to those who have no faith in me to follow my friend Shaukat Ali. They need not believe in the purity of my motives, but must clearly recognize that there can be no violence simultaneously with non-cooperation. The greatest obstacle to the launching of all-out non-cooperation is the fear of violence breaking out. Those who are ready with arms or are eager to be so should also put them by while non-cooperation is going on.

"To me, on the day when brute force gains ascendancy in India all distinction of East and West, of ancient and modern, will have disappeared. That day will be the day of my test. I take pride in looking upon India as my country because I believe that she has it in her to demonstrate to the world the supremacy of soul-force. When India accepts the supremacy of brute force, I should no longer be happy to call her my motherland. It is my belief that my *dharma* recognizes no limits of spheres of duty or of geographical boundaries. I pray to God that I may then be able to prove that my *dharma* takes no thought of my person or is not restricted to a particular field."

"It [*Satyagraha*] is a force that may be used by individuals as well as by communities. It may be used as well in political as in domestic affairs. Its universal applicability is a demonstration of its permanence and invincibility. It can be used alike by men, women and children. It is totally untrue to say that it is a force to be used only by the weak so long as they are not capable of meeting violence by violence."

"In this age of wonders no one will say that a thing or an idea is worthless because it is new. To say it is impossible because it is difficult, is again not in consonance with the spirit of the age. Things undreamt of are daily being seen, the impossible is ever becoming possible. We are constantly being astonished these days at the amazing discoveries in the field of violence. But I maintain that far more undreamt of and seemingly impossible discoveries will be made in the field of nonviolence."

"Nonviolence is the greatest force at the disposal of mankind. It is mightier than the mightiest weapon of destruction devised by the ingenuity of man."

"We have to make truth and nonviolence not matters for mere individual practice but for practice by groups and communities and nations. That at any rate is my dream. I shall live and die in trying to realize it. My faith helps me to discover new truths every day."

FAITH

"Man often becomes what he believes himself to be. If I keep on saying to myself that I cannot do a certain thing, it is possible that I may end by really becoming incapable of doing it. On the contrary, if I have the belief that I can do it, I shall surely acquire the capacity to do it even if I may not have it at the beginning."

"I believe in God, not only as a theory but as a fact more real than that of life itself."

"If we have listening ears, God speaks to us in our own language, whatever that language be."

"The Bible is as much of a book of religion with me as the *Gita* and the *Koran.*"

"Religion is the tie that binds one to one's Creator, and whilst the body perishes, as it has to, religion persists even after death."

"I claim that human mind or human society is not divided into watertight compartments called social, political and religious. All act and react upon one another."

"I do not believe that the spiritual law works on a field of its own. On the contrary, it expresses itself only through the ordinary activities of life. It thus affects the economic, the social and the political fields."

"Religions are different roads converging upon the same point. What does it matter that we take different roads so long as we reach the same goal?"

"To see the universal and all-pervading Spirit of Truth face to face one must be able to love the meanest of creation as oneself. And a man who aspires after that cannot afford to keep out of any field of life. That is why my devotion to Truth has drawn me into the field of politics; and I can say without the slightest hesitation, and yet in all humility, that those who say that religion has nothing to do with politics do not know what religion means."

"Prayer is not asking. It is a longing of the soul. It is daily admission of one's weakness . . . It is better in prayer to have a heart without words than words without a heart."

"Prayer is the key of the morning and the bolt of the evening."

"A man who throws himself on God ceases to fear man."

"'Do not worry in the least about yourself, leave all worry to God,'—this appears to be the commandment in all religions.

"This need not frighten anyone. He who devotes himself to service with a clear conscience, will day by day grasp the necessity for it in greater measure, and will continually grow richer in faith. The path of service can hardly be trodden by one who is not prepared to renounce self-interest, and to recognize the conditions of his birth. Consciously or unconsciously, every one of us does render some service or other. If we cultivate the habit of doing this service deliberately, our desire for service will steadily grow stronger, and will make not only for our own happiness but that of the world at large."

"If we will take care of today, God will take care of the morrow."

"The truth is that God is the force. He is the essence of life. He is pure and undefiled consciousness. He is eternal."

"God answers prayer in His own way, not ours."

"A man of faith does not bargain or stipulate with God."

"God alone is immortal, imperishable."

"Cowardice is not a sign of belief in God."

"What is faith worth if it is not translated into action?"

"I believe in the fundamental truth of all great religions of the world. I believe that they are all God-given and I believe that they were necessary for the people to whom these religions were revealed. And I believe that if only we could all of us read the scriptures of the different faiths from the standpoint of the followers of these faiths, we should find that they were at the bottom all one and were all helpful to one another."

"A correspondent says in substance:

'Individual *ahimsa* I can understand. Corporate *ahimsa* between friends is also intelligible. But you talk of *ahimsa* towards avowed enemies. This is like a mirage. It will be a mercy if you give up this obstinacy of yours. If you do not, you will forfeit the esteem you enjoy. What is worse, your being considered a *Mahatma* misleads many credulous persons to their own and society's harm.'

"That nonviolence which only an individual can use is not of much use in terms of society. Man is a social being. His accomplishments to be of use must be such as any person with sufficient diligence can attain. That which can be exercised only among friends is of value only as a spark of nonviolence. It cannot merit the appelation of *ahimsa*. 'Enmity vanishes before *ahimsa*' is a great aphorism. It means that the greatest enmity requires an equal measure of *ahimsa* for its abatement. Cultivation of this virtue may need long practice, even extending to several births. It does not become useless on that account. Travelling along the route, the pilgrim will meet richer experiences from day to day so that he may have a glimpse of the beauty he is destined to see at the top. This will add to his zest. No one is entitled to infer from this that the path will be a continuous carpet of roses without thorns. A poet has sung that the way to reach God accrues only to the very brave, never to the faint-

hearted. The atmosphere today is so much saturated with poison that one refuses to recollect the wisdom of the ancients and to perceive the varied little experiences of *ahimsa* in action. 'A bad turn is neutralized by a good' is a wise saying of daily experience in practice. Why can we not see that if the sum total of the world's activities was destructive, it would have come to an end long ago? Love, otherwise *ahimsa,* sustains this planet of ours.

"This much must be admitted. The precious grace of life has to be strenuously cultivated, naturally so because it is uplifting. Descent is easy, not so ascent. A large majority of us being undisciplined, our daily experience is that of fighting or swearing at one another on the slightest pretext.

"This, the richest grace of *ahimsa,* will descend easily upon the owner of hard discipline."

"Faith is a function of the heart. It must be enforced by reason. The two are not antagonistic as some think. The more intense one's faith is, the more it whets one's reason. When faith becomes blind it dies."

"Truth is God and God is Truth."

"The sum total of all that lives is God. We may not be God but we are of God even as a little drop of water is of the ocean."

"A man with a grain of faith in God never loses hope, because he ever believes in the ultimate triumph of Truth."

"Close the day with prayer so that you may have a peaceful night free from dreams and nightmares."

"When I admire the wonder of a sunset or the beauty of the moon, my soul expands in worship of the Creator."

PEACE

"The way of peace is the way of truth. Truthfulness is even more important than peacefulness. Indeed, lying is the mother of violence. A truthful man cannot long remain violent. He will perceive in the course of his search that he has no need to be violent and he will further discover that so long as there is the slightest trace of violence in him, he will fail to find the truth he is searching.

"There is no halfway between truth and nonviolence on the one hand and untruth and violence on the other. We may never be strong enough to be entirely nonviolent in thought, word and deed. But we must keep nonviolence as our goal and make steady progress towards it. The attainment of freedom, whether for a man, a nation or the world, must be in exact proportion to the attainment of nonviolence by each. Let those, therefore, who believe in nonviolence as the only method of achieving real freedom, keep the lamp of nonviolence as the only method of achieving real freedom, keep the lamp of nonviolence burning bright in the midst of the present impenetrable gloom. The truth of a few will count, the untruth of millions will vanish even like chaff before a whiff of wind."

"The better mind of the world desires today not absolutely independent states warring one against another, but a federation of friendly interdependent states."

"Interdependence is and ought to be as much the ideal of man as self-sufficiency. Man is a social being. Without interrelation with society he cannot realize its oneness with the universe or suppress his egotism."

"It is impossible for one to be internationalist without being a nationalist. Internationalism is possible only when nationalism becomes a fact, i.e., when peoples belonging to different countries have organized themselves and are able to act as one man."

"What I want you to understand is the message of Asia. It is not to be learnt through the Western spectacles or by imitating the atom bomb. If you want to give a message to the West, it must be the message of love and the message of truth. I do not want merely to appeal to your head. I want to capture your heart.

"In this age of democracy, in this age of awakening of the poorest of the poor, you can redeliver this message with the greatest emphasis. You will complete the conquest of the West not through vengeance because you have been exploited, but with real understanding. I am sanguine if all of you put your hearts together—not merely heads—to understand the secret of the message these wise men of the East have left to us, and if we really become worthy of that great message, the conquest of the West will be completed. This conquest will be loved by the West itself.

"The West is today pining for wisdom. It is despairing of a multiplication of the atom bombs, because atom bombs mean utter destruction not merely of the West but of the whole world, as if the prophesy of the Bible is going to be fulfilled and there is to be a perfect deluge. It is up to you to tell the world of its wickedness and sin—that is the heritage your teachers and my teachers have taught Asia."

"If there were no greed, there would be no occasion for armaments. The principle of nonviolence necessitates complete abstention from exploitation in any form."

"As soon as the spirit of exploitation is gone, armaments will be felt as a positive unbearable burden. Real disarmament cannot come unless the nations of the world cease to exploit one another."

"The fashion nowadays is to take for granted that whatever America and England are doing is good enough for us. But the figures given by the writer of the cost to America of her armament are too terrible to contemplate. War has become a matter of money and resourcefulness in inventing weapons of destruction. It is no longer a matter of personal bravery or endurance. To compass the destruction of men, women and children, it might be enough for me to press a button and drop poison on them in a second.

"Do we wish to copy this method of defending ourselves? Even if we do, have we the financial ability? We complain of an ever growing military expenditure. But if we would copy America or

England, we would have to increase the burden tenfold.

"The nation cannot be kept on the nonviolent path by violence. It must grow from within to the state it may aspire to. The question therefore for us to consider is, 'What is our immediate aspiration?' Do we first want to copy the Western nations and then in the dim and distant future after having gone through the agony retrace our steps? Or do we want to strike out on an original path and thereby win and assert our freedom?

"Here there is no question of compromises with cowardice. Either we train and arm ourselves for destruction, but in self-defense, and in the process train for suffering too, or we merely prepare ourselves for suffering for defending the country or delivering it from domination. In either case bravery is indispensable. In the first case personal bravery is not of such importance as in the second. In the second case too we shall perhaps never be able to do without violence altogether. But violence then will be subservient to nonviolence and will always be a diminishing factor in national life.

"If the mad race for armaments continues it is bound to result in a slaughter such as has never occurred in history. If there is a victor left the very victory will be a living death for the nation that emerges victorious."

"At the present moment, though the national creed is one of nonviolence, in thought and word at least we seem to be drifting towards violence. Impatience pervades the atmosphere. We are restrained from violence through our weakness. What is wanted is a deliberate giving up of violence out of strength. To be able to do this requires imagination coupled with a penetrating study of the world drift. Today the superficial glamour of the West dazzles us, and we mistake for progress the giddy dance which engages us from day to day. We refuse to see that it is surely leading us to death. Above all we must recognize that to compete with the Western nations on their terms is to court suicide. Whereas if we realize that notwithstanding the seeming supremacy of violence it is the moral force that governs the universe, we should train for nonviolence with the fullest faith in its limitless possibilities. Everybody recognises that if a nonviolent atmosphere had been maintained in 1922* we could have completely gained our end. Even as it is, we had a striking demonstration of the efficacy of nonviolence, crude though it was, and the substance of *swaraj* then gained has never been lost. The paralyzing fear that had possessed the nation before the advent of *satyagraha* has gone once for all. In my opinion therefore nonviolence is a matter of patient training. If we are to be saved and are to make a substantial contribution to the world's progress, ours must emphatically and predominantly be the way of peace."

"It may be long before the law of love will be recognized in internal affairs. The machineries of governments stand between and hide the hearts of one people from those of another."

---

*In 1922 Gandhi started a civil disobedience campaign near Bombay. He was charged with sedition for three articles he wrote for the weekly he edited, *Young India*. He was arrested on 10 March 1922 and was imprisoned until mid-1924.

"Some time ago I suggested the formation of a peace brigade whose members would risk their lives in dealing with riots, especially communal. The idea was that this brigade should substitute for the police and even the military. This reads ambitiously. The achievement may prove impossible. Yet, if the Congress is to succeed in its nonviolent struggle, it must develop the power to deal peacefully with such situations. Communal riots are engineered by politically minded men. Many of those who take part in them are under the influence of the latter. Surely it should not be beyond the wit of Congressmen to devise a method or methods of avoiding ugly communal situations by peaceful means. I say this irrespective of whether there is or there is not a communal pact. It cannot be that any party seeks to force a pact by violent means. Even if such a pact were a possibility, it would not be worth the paper on which it might be written. For behind such a pact there will be no communal understanding. What is more, even after a pact is arrived at it would be too much to expect that there would never be any communal riots.

"Let us, therefore, see what qualifications a member of the contemplated peace brigade should possess.

"1. He or she must have a living faith in nonviolence. This is impossible without a living faith in

God. A nonviolent man can do nothing save by the power and grace of God. Without it he won't have the courage to die without anger, without fear and without retaliation. Such courage comes from the belief that God sits in the hearts of all, and that there should be no fear in the presence of God. The knowledge of the omnipresence of God also means respect for the lives of even those who may be called opponents or goondas. This contemplated intervention is a process of stilling the fury of man when the brute in him gets the mastery over him.

"2. This messenger of peace must have equal regard for all the principal religions of the earth. Thus, if he is Hindu, he will respect the other faiths current in India. He must, therefore, possess a knowledge of the general principles of the different faiths professed in the country.

"3. Generally speaking this work of peace can only be done by local men in their own localities.

"4. The work can be done singly or in groups. Therefore, no one need wait for companions. Nevertheless one would naturally seek companions in one's own locality and form a local brigade.

"5. This messenger of peace will cultivate, through personal service, contacts with the people in his locality or chosen circle, so that when he appears to deal with ugly situations, he does not descend upon the members of a riotous assembly as an utter stranger liable to be looked upon as a suspect or an unwelcome visitor.

"6. Needless to say, a peace-bringer must have a character beyond reproach and must be known for his strict impartiality.

"7. Generally there are previous warnings of coming storms. Where these are known, the peace brigade will not wait till the conflagration breaks out, but will try to handle the situation in anticipation.

"8. Whilst, if the movement spreads, it might be well if there are some full-time workers, it is not absolutely necessary that there should be. The idea is to have as many good and true men and women as possible. These can be had only if volunteers are drawn from those who are engaged in various walks of life but have leisure enough to cultivate friendly relations with the people living in their circle and otherwise possess the qualifications required of a member of the peace brigade.

"9. There should be a distinctive dress worn by the members of the contemplated brigade so that in course of time they will be recognized without the slightest difficulty.

"These are but general suggestions. Each centre can work out its own constitution on the basis here suggested.

"Lest false hopes may be raised, I must warn workers against entertaining the hope that I can play any active part in the formation of peace brigades. I have not the health, energy or time for it. I find it hard enough to cope with the tasks I dare not shirk. I can only guide and make suggestions through correspondence or these columns. Therefore let those who appreciate the idea and feel they have the ability, take the initiative themselves. I know that the proposed brigade has great possibilities, and that the idea behind it is quite capable of being worked out in practice."

"I have found that life persists in the midst of destruction and therefore there must be a higher law than that of destruction. Only under that law would a well-ordered society be intelligible and life worth living."

(Writing in the Harijan *of 10 February 1946, Gandhi asked: "There have been cataclysmic changes in the world. Do I still adhere to my faith in truth and nonviolence? Has not the atom bomb exploded that faith?" And his answer was in the negative. Speaking at Poona on 3 March 1946, he raised a basic question: "Has not the atom bomb proved the futility of all violence?" His reflections on this problem are of a profound nature. Speaking at New Delhi on 24 September 1946 he observed: "Nonviolence . . . is the only thing that the atom bomb cannot destroy. I did not move a muscle when I first heard that the atom bomb had wiped out Hiroshima. On the contrary, I said to myself, Unless now the world adopts nonviolence, it will spell certain suicide for mankind." The following was Gandhi's speech at Poona on 1 July 1946 on the atom bomb.)*

"It has been suggested by American friends that the atom bomb will bring in *ahimsa* (nonviolence) as nothing else can. It will, if it is meant that its destructive power will so disgust the world that it will turn it away from violence for the time being. This is very like a man glutting himself with dainties to the point of nausea and turning away from them only to return with redoubled zeal after the effect of nausea is well over. Precisely in the same manner will the world return to violence with renewed zeal after the effect of disgust is worn out.

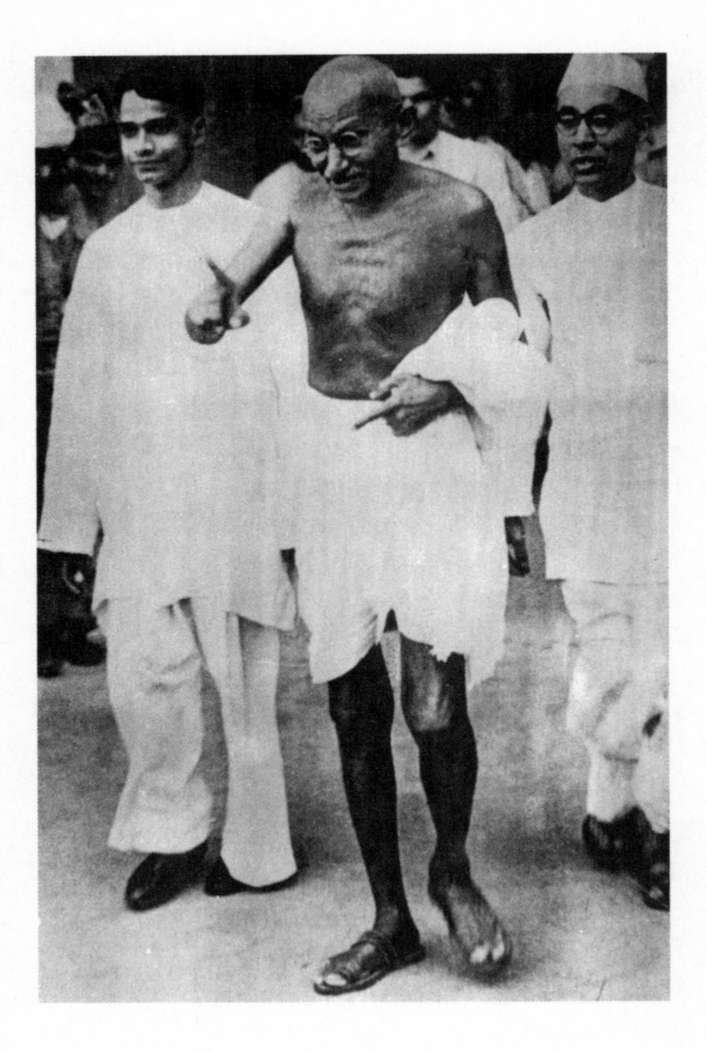

"Often does good come out of evil. But that is God's, not man's plan. Man knows that only evil can come out of evil, as good out of good.

"That atomic energy though harnessed by American scientists and army men for destructive purposes may be utilised by other scientists for humanitarian purposes is undoubtedly within the realm of possibility. But that is not what was meant by my American friends. They were not so simple as to put a question which connoted an obvious truth. An incendiary uses fire for his destructive and nefarious purpose, a housewife makes daily use of it in preparing nourishing food for mankind.

"So far as I can see, the atomic bomb has deadened the finest feeling that has sustained mankind for ages. There used to be the so-called laws of war which made it tolerable. Now we know the naked truth. War knows no law except that of might. The atom bomb brought an empty victory to the allied armies but it resulted for the time being in destroying the soul of Japan. What has happened to the soul of the destroying nation is yet too early to see. Forces of nature act in a mysterious manner. We can but solve the mystery by deducing the unknown result from the known results of similar events. A slaveholder cannot hold a slave without putting himself or his deputy in the cage holding the slave. Let no one run away with the idea that I wish to put in a defence of Japanese misdeeds in pursuance of Japan's unworthy ambition. The difference was only one of degree. I assume that Japan's greed was more unworthy. But the greater unworthiness conferred no right on the less unworthy of destroying without mercy men, women and children of Japan in a particular area.

"The moral to be legitimately drawn from the supreme tragedy of the bomb is that it will not be destroyed by counter-bombs even as violence cannot be by counter-violence. Mankind has to get out of violence only through nonviolence. Hatred can be overcome only by love. Counter-hatred only increases the surface as well as the depth of hatred. I am aware that I am repeating what I have many times stated before and practised to the best of my ability and capacity. What I first stated was itself nothing new. It was as old as the hills. Only I recited no copybook maxim but definitely announced what I believed in every fibre of my being. Sixty years of practise in various walks of life has only enriched the belief which experience of friends has fortified. It is however the central truth by which one can stand alone without flinching. I believe in what Max Müller* said years ago,

---

*Max Müller, 1823–1900: German philologist and Orientalist. Author of many works on Indian religion and philosophy.

namely, that truth needed to be repeated as long as there were men who disbelieved it."

"If we are to reach real peace in this world and if we are to carry on a real war against war, we shall have to begin with children; and if they grow up in their natural innocence, we won't have to struggle; we won't have to pass fruitless idle resolutions, but we shall go from love to love and peace to peace, until at last all the corners of the world are covered with that peace and love for which consciously or unconsciously the whole world is hungering."

"I want to realize brotherhood or identity not merely with the beings called human, but I want to realize identity with all life, even with such beings as crawl on earth."

"I do believe that all God's creatures have the right to live as much as we have. Instead of prescribing the killing of the so-called injurious fellow creatures of ours as a duty, if men of knowledge had devoted their gift to discovering ways of dealing with them otherwise than by killing them, we would be living in a world befitting our status as men—animals endowed with reason and the power of choosing between good and evil, right and wrong, violence and nonviolence, truth and untruth."

NOTES

Most of the writings appearing in this collection were originally published in Young India *and* Harijan *(its Gujarati counterpart), weekly periodicals edited by Gandhi. These were forums for Gandhi and the Indian civil disobedience and independence movements. In India,* harijan *referred to the "untouchable" caste, but Gandhi translated the phrase as "children of God." Additional text has been taken from Gandhi's autobiography,* The Story of My Experiments with Truth *(1927).*

The writings included in this book span a period of over four decades. About their continuity, Gandhi wrote:

"My writings should be cremated with my body. What I have done will endure, not what I have said and written. I have often said recently that even if all our scripture were to perish, one *mantra* of *Ishopanishad* was enough to declare the essence of Hinduism, but even that one verse will be of no avail if there is no one to live it. Even so what I have said and written is useful only to the extent that it has helped you to assimilate the great principles of truth and *ahimsa*. If you have not assimilated them, then my writings will be of no use to you."

"At the time of writing I never think of what I have said before. My aim is not to be consistent with my previous statements on a given question, but to be consistent with truth as it may present itself to me at a given moment. The result has been that I have grown from truth to truth; I have saved my memory an undue strain; and what is more, whenever I have been obliged to compare my writing even of fifty years ago with the latest, I have discovered no inconsistency between the two. But friends who observe inconsistency will do well to take the meaning that my latest writing may yield unless, of course, they prefer the old. But before making the choice they should try to see if there is not an underlying and abiding consistency between the two seeming inconsistencies."

Concerning his own achievements, Gandhi wrote:

"Let Gandhism be destroyed if it stands for error. Truth and *ahimsa* will never be destroyed, but if Gandhism is another name for sectarianism, it deserves to be destroyed. If I were to know, after my death, that what I stood for had degenerated into sectarianism, I should be deeply pained. We have to work away silently. Let no one say that he is a follower of Gandhi. It is enough that I should be my own follower. I know what an inadequate follower I am of myself, for I cannot live up to the convictions I stand for."

Gandhi's concepts of *ahimsa* and *satyagraha* are central to his writings. Their effectiveness in improving the conditions of Indians in South Africa and in seeking independence for India were further proof that there are stronger forces at humankind's disposal than violence.

The Sanskrit word *ahimsa* is at the foundation of *satyagraha*. It literally means "lacking any desire to kill." This is considered to be the natural state of the human spirit, which can be realized or uncovered by practicing true love toward all living things. To love those who are considered to be your enemies is the natural progression of *ahimsa*. Unlike the word "nonviolence," with which it is often paired, *ahimsa* implies a state in which no violence—of thought or action—exists. In such a state, there is only love. To practice *ahimsa* requires strength; a person must be willing to maintain a condition of *ahimsa* even in the face of tremendous adversity.

Gandhi invented the word *satyagraha* in South Africa in 1908 to distinguish it from such phrases as "civil disobedience" and "passive resistance." It is built upon the words *satya* (truth) and *agraha* (firmness). Gandhi viewed truth as an expression of love, and firmness as an expression of strength. Gandhi recognized the subjective nature of "truth" for mankind: "truth" was often influenced by a person's own self-interests. "Firmness," the denial of self-interest, was Gandhi's solution to this subjectivity. This was not a passive solution. To deny one's material wants as well as any emotions that run counter to a spirit of *ahimsa* required strength. By following this path, the *satyagrahi* (practitioner of *satyagraha*) is able to release a force stronger than any weapon. It is a force of intense love born out of an absence of self-interest. It is an active seeking of the truth, devoid of hostility, anger and violence, which allows the victim to view himself as one with his attacker.

Gandhi defined *satyagraha* as "soul-force," which emerges through the uncovering of the true human spirit.

GLOSSARY

brahmachary Someone who has taken a vow of sexual abstinence.

chapati A flat Indian bread.

charkha Indian spinning wheel. Symbol of Gandhi's effort to return India to self-sufficiency. It appears on the Indian national flag.

dharma In Hinduism, the religious and ethical rights and duties of each individual. Sometimes interpreted as simple virtue or right conduct, sometimes as ordained or pre-ordained duty.

Gita Bhagavad-Gita, "Song of the Blessed One." One of the most important religious books of Hinduism.

Koran The sacred book of Islam.

Mahatma Hindi for "great soul."

mantra In Hinduism, a word or phrase to be recited or sung repetitively.

mobocracy Rule by the mob.

rishi An inspired Hindu poet or sage.

swaraj Independence. Long used to call for complete independence from Britain as opposed to various schemes of autonomy.

vaid Medicine prescribed by a Hindu medicine man, or *vaidya*.

AFTERWORD

MOHANDAS GANDHI (1869–1948)

In an age of empire and military might, he proved that the powerless had power and that force of arms would not forever prevail against force of spirit.

The Mahatma, the Great Soul, endures in the best part of our minds, where our ideals are kept: the embodiment of human rights and the creed of nonviolence. Mohandas Karamchand Gandhi is something else, an eccentric of complex, contradictory and exhausting character most of us hardly know. It is fashionable at this fin de siècle to use the man to tear down the hero, to expose human pathologies at the expense of larger-than-life achievements. No myth raking can rob Gandhi of his moral force or diminish the remarkable importance of this scrawny little man. For the twentieth century—and surely for the ones to follow—it is the towering myth of the Mahatma that matters.

Consciously or not, every oppressed people or group with a cause has practiced what Gandhi preached. Sixties kids like me were his disciples when we went South in the Freedom Summer to sit in for civil rights and when we paraded through the streets of America to stop the war in Vietnam. Our passionate commitment, nonviolent activism, willingness to accept punishment for civil disobedience were lessons he taught. Martin Luther King, Jr. learned them; so did Nelson Mandela, Lech Wałesa, Aung

San Suu Kyi—the unknown Chinese who defied the tanks in 1989 and the environmental marchers in Seattle a few weeks ago.

It may be that this most Indian of leaders, revered as Bapuji, or Father of the Nation, means more now to the world at large. Foreigners don't have to wrestle with the confusion Indians feel today as they judge whether their nation has kept faith with his vision. For the rest of us, his image offers something much simpler—a shining set of ideals to emulate. Individual freedom. Political liberty. Social justice. Nonviolent protest. Passive resistance. Religious tolerance. His work and his spirit awakened the twentieth century to ideas that serve as a moral beacon for all epochs.

Half a century after his death, most of us know little of Gandhi's real history or how the Mahatma in our minds came to be. Hundreds of biographies uncritically canonize him. Winston Churchill scorned him as a half-naked fakir stirring up sedition. His generation knew him as a radical political agitator; ours shrugs off a holy man with romantic notions of a pure, pre-industrial life. There is no either-or. The saint and the politician inhabited the same slender frame, each nourishing the other. His struggle for a nation's rights was one and the same with his struggle for individual salvation.

The flesh-and-blood Gandhi was a most unlikely saint. Just conjure up his portrait: a skinny, bent figure, nut brown and naked except for a white loincloth, cheap spectacles perched on his nose, frail hand grasping a tall bamboo staff. This was one of the century's great revolutionaries? Yet this strange figure swayed millions with his hypnotic spell. His garb was the perfect uniform for the kind of revolutionary he was, wielding weapons of prayer and nonviolence more powerful than guns.

Saints are hard to live with, and this one's personal habits were decidedly odd. Mondays were "days of silence," when he refused to speak. A devoted vegetarian, he indulged in faddish dietetic experiments that sometimes came near to killing him. He eschewed all spices as a discipline of the senses. He napped every day with a mud poultice on abdomen and brow. He was so insistent on absolute regularity in his daily regimen that he safety-pinned a watch to his homespun *dhoti,* synchronized with the clock at his ashram. He scheduled his bowel movements for twenty minutes morning and afternoon. "The bathroom is a temple," he said, and anyone was welcome to chat with him there. He had a cleansing enema every night.

Gandhi bathed in water but used ashes instead of soap and had himself shaved with a dull straight razor because new blades were too expensive. He was always sweeping up excrement that others left around. Cleanliness, he believed, was godliness. But his passion for sanitation was not just finicky hygiene. He wanted to teach Indian villagers that human and animal filth caused most of the disease in the land.

Every afternoon, Gandhi did an hour or two of spinning on his little handwheel, sometimes four hundred yards at a sitting. "I am spinning the destiny of India," he would say. The thread went to make cloth for his followers, and he hoped his example would convince Indians that homespun could free them from dependence on foreign products. But the real point of the spinning was to teach appreciation for manual labor, restore self-respect lost to colonial subjugation and cultivate inner strength.

The man was not unaware of his legend in the making—or the ninety-plus volumes that would eventually be needed to preserve his words. Everything Gandhi ever said and did was recorded by legions of secretaries. Then he insisted on going over their notes and choosing the version he liked best. "I want only one gospel in my life," he said.

A strange amalgam of beliefs formed the complicated core of Gandhism. History will merely smile at his railing against Western ways, industrialism and material pleasures. He never stopped calling for a nation that would turn its back on technology to prosper through village self-sufficiency, but not even the Mahatma could hold back progress. Yet many today share his uneasiness with the way mechanization and materialism sicken the human spirit.

More central and even more controversial was Gandhi's cult of celibacy. At thirteen, he dutifully married and came quickly to lust for his wife, Kasturba. At sixteen he left his dying father's side to make love to her. His father died that night, and Gandhi could never forgive himself the "double shame." He neglected and even humiliated Kasturba most of his life and only after her death realized she was "the warp and woof of my life." At thirty-six, convinced that sex was the basis of all impulses that must be mastered if man was to reach Truth, he renounced it. An aspirant to a godly life must observe the Hindu practice of *Brahmacharya,* or celibacy, as a means of self-control and a way to devote all energy to public service. Gandhi spent years testing his self-discipline by sleeping beside young women. He evidently cared little about any psychological damage to the women involved. He also expected his four sons to be as self-denying as he was.

Gandhi sought God, not orthodoxy. His daily prayers mixed traditional Hindu venerations with Buddhist chants, readings from the Koran, a Zoroastrian verse or two and the Christian hymn *Lead, Kindly Light.* That eclecticism reflected his great tolerance for all religions, one of his holiest—and least respected—precepts. "Truth," he preached, "is God," but he could never persuade India's warring religious sects to agree. His spiritual mentors were just as broad—Jesus, Buddha, Socrates, his mother. Gandhi later said his formative childhood impression was of her "saintliness" and her devout asceticism infused his soul. The family's brand of Hinduism schooled him in the sacredness of all God's creatures.

While studying in England to be a lawyer, he first read the Bible and the Bhagavad Gita, the Hindu religious poem that became his "spiritual dictionary." For Gandhi, the epic was a clarion call to the soul to undertake the battle of righteousness. It taught him to renounce personal desires not by withdrawal from the world but by devotion to the service of his fellow man. In the Christian New Testament he found the stirrings of passive resistance in the words of the Sermon on the Mount.

Those credos came together in the two principles that ruled his public life: what he called *satyagraha,* the force of truth and love; and the ancient Hindu ideal of *ahimsa,* or nonviolence to all living things. He first put those principles to political work in South Africa, where he had gone to practice law and tasted raw discrimination. Traveling to Johannesburg in a first-class train compartment, he was ordered to move to the "colored" cars in the rear. When he refused, he was hauled off the train and left to spend a freezing night in the station. The next day he was humiliated and cuffed by the white driver of a stagecoach. The experience steeled his resolve to fight for social justice.

In 1906, confronting a government move to fingerprint all Indians, Gandhi countered with a new idea—"passive resistance," securing political rights through personal suffering and the power of truth and love. "Indians," he wrote, "will stagger humanity without shedding a drop of blood." He failed to provoke legal changes, and Indians gained little more than a newfound self-respect. But Gandhi understood the universal application of his crusade. Even his principal adversary, the Afrikaner leader Jan Smuts, recognized the power of his idea: "Men like him redeem us from a sense of commonplace and futility."

South Africa was dress rehearsal for Gandhi's great cause, independence for India. From the day he arrived back home at forty-five, he dedicated himself to *Hind swaraj,* Indian self-rule. More than independence, it meant a utopian blend of national liberty, individual self-reliance and social justice. Freedom entailed individual emancipation as well, the search for nobility of soul through self-discipline and denial. Most ordinary Indians, though, were just looking for an end to colonial rule. While his peace-and-love homilies may not have swayed them, they followed him because he made the British tremble.

"Action is my domain," he said. "It's not what I say but what I do that matters." He quickly became the commanding figure of the movement and brooked no challenge to his ultimate leadership. The force of his convictions transformed the Indian National Congress from upper-class movement to mass crusade. He made his little spinning wheel a physical bond between elite and illiterate when both donned the *khadi* cloth. Despite the country's proclivities for ethnic and religious strife, he inspired legions of Indians to join peaceful protests that made a mockery of empire.

In the next thirty-three years, he led three major crusades to undermine the power and moral defenses of the British Raj. In 1919 to 1922 he mustered widespread nonviolent strikes, then a campaign of peaceful non-cooperation, urging Indians to boycott anything British—schools, courts, goods, even the English language. He believed mass non-cooperation would achieve independence within a year. Instead, it degenerated into bloody rioting, and British soldiers turned their guns on a crowd in Amritsar, massacring four hundred. Gandhi called his underestimating of the violence inside Indian society his "Himalayan blunder." Still, villagers mobbed him wherever he went, calling him Mahatma. By 1922, thirty thousand followers had been jailed, and Gandhi ordered civil disobedience. The British slowed the momentum by jailing him for twenty-two months.

Gandhi was never a man to give up. On 12 March 1930, he launched his most brilliant stroke, national defiance of the law forbidding Indians to make their own salt. With seventy-eight followers, he set out for the coast to make salt until the law was repealed. By the time he reached the sea, people all across the land had joined in. Civil disobedience spread until Gandhi was arrested again. Soon more than sixty thousand Indians filled the jails, and Britain was shamed by the gentle power of the old man and his unresisting supporters. Though Gandhi had been elected to no office and represented no government, the Viceroy soon began negotiating with him.

World War II caught him by surprise. The unremitting pacifist did not grasp the evil of Hitler because he thought no man beyond redemption. He deeply offended Jews when he counseled them to follow the path of nonviolence. Gandhi did not want Britain's defeat, but recognized a political opportunity. In late 1940 he agreed to a modest campaign of individual civil disobedience he intended to be largely symbolic.

But other politicians pressed hard for nonviolent mass struggle against a Raj dangerously weakened by the threat of Japanese invasion. In 1942 Gandhi reluctantly endorsed the Quit India plan, calling on London for Indian independence "before dawn, if it could be had." He and the Congress leaders were arrested and jailed. Huge demonstrations soon flared into rioting and revolt. Mobs attacked any symbol of British power, and the disorder cut off British communications to its armies at the frontier. Government forces struck back hard, and nearly one thousand Indians were killed before the uprising flamed out. Gandhi was finally freed on 5 May 1944. He had spent 2,338 days of his 74 years imprisoned.

By war's end, Britain was ready to let India go. But the moment of Gandhi's greatest triumph, on 15 August 1947, was also the hour of his defeat. India gained freedom but lost unity when Britain granted independence on the same day it created the new Muslim state of Pakistan. Partition dishonored Gandhi's sect-blind creed. "There is no message at all," he said that day and turned to fasting and prayer.

At seventy-seven, he despaired that "my life's work seems to be over." Had liberty been won by the long years of peaceful and moral coercion or the violent spasm of Quit India? Resentment of Britain had been replaced by religious hatred. The killing before partition made it inevitable, and the slaughter afterward trampled on his appeals to tolerance and trust. All the village pilgrimages he made in 1946 and 1947 could not stop Muslims and Hindus from killing one another. All the famous fasts he undertook could not persuade them to live permanently in harmony. He blamed himself when Indians rejected the nonviolence he had made a way of life.

Assassination made a martyr of the apostle of nonviolence. The Hindu fanatic who fired three bullets into Gandhi at point-blank range on 30 January 1948 blamed him for letting Muslims steal part of the Hindu nation, for not hating Muslims. Not long before, Gandhi had noted his new irrelevance. "Everybody is eager to garland my photos," he said. "But nobody wants to follow my advice."

He was both right and wrong. Interest in the flesh-and-blood Mohandas Karamchand has faded away. We revere the Mahatma while ignoring half of what he taught. His backward, romantic vision of a simple society seems woolly minded. Much of his ascetic personal philosophy has lost meaning for later generations. Global politics have little place today for his absolute pacificism or gentle tolerance.

Yet Gandhi is that rare great man held in universal esteem, a figure lifted from history to moral icon. The fundamental message of his transcendent personality persists. He stamped his ideas on history, igniting three of the century's great revolutions—against colonialism, racism, violence. His concept of nonviolent resistance liberated one nation and sped the end of colonial empires around the world. His marches and fasts fired the imagination of oppressed people everywhere. Like the millions of Indians who pressed around his funeral cortege seeking *darshan*—contact with his sanctity—millions more have sought freedom and justice under the Mahatma's guiding light. He shines as a conscience for the world. The saint and the politician go hand in hand, proclaiming the power of love, peace and freedom.

—JOHANNA MCGEARY, *Time* magazine Senior Foreign Correspondent, contributed this essay to *Time* magazine's *Person of the Millennium* issue (31 December 1999), in which Gandhi was honored for his life and work in the twentieth century.

Ms. McGeary has won three Overseas Press Club awards for foreign reporting and is the recipient of the 1997 Overseas Press Club Certificate of Excellence in Reporting award.

CHRONOLOGY

MOHANDAS KARAMCHAND GANDHI
1869–1948

1869 Born on October 2 to Hindu parents in Porbander, Kathiawar, India. He is the youngest son of Karamchand Kaba Gandhi and his fourth wife, Putli.

1883 Enters an arranged marriage with thirteen-year-old Kasturba Makanji.

1888 Sails to England on September 4 to study law.

1890 Graduates law school in June.

1891 Called to the Bar on June 10. Sails for India on June 12. He has several jobs practicing law but is unsuccessful in each.

1893 Travels to South Africa in April to represent Dada Abdullah and Company, an Indian Moslem trading firm.

1894 In August, he organizes the Indian Natal Congress, which works to improve the rights of immigrant Indians. In September, he becomes the first Indian to be enrolled as an Advocate of Supreme Court of Natal.

1897 After a brief trip to India in 1896, he returns to South Africa with his wife and children. He is mobbed on landing at Durban, South Africa, on January 13, by crowds angered by his criticism of indentured Indian labor conditions in South Africa. He declines to press charges against his assailants.

1899 Raises Indian Ambulance Corps for British in Boer War. He is awarded a War Medal.

1901 Returns home to India to practice law.

1902 Returns to South Africa in November to champion Indian cause in Transvaal.

1903 Enrolls as an attorney of Supreme Court of Transvaal. He founds the Transvaal British Indian Association. Begins publishing the newspaper *Indian Opinion* in June.

1904 Founds Phoenix Settlement, the first of Gandhi's self-contained communities (or *ashrams*), near Durban.

1906 In September, leads first *satyagraha* (active, nonviolent resistance) campaign in protest of a proposed Asiatic ordinance directed against Indian immigrants in Transvaal.

1907 In June, organizes *satyagraha* against compulsory registration of Asiatics (the Black Act).

1908 Stands trial for instigating *satyagraha* and is sentenced to two months' imprisonment in Johannesburg jail (his first imprisonment). He is released after accepting a promise from Boer General Jan Christiaan Smuts that the ordinance will be repealed. After Smuts breaks the agreement, Gandhi organizes a second *satyagraha* campaign that begins with a bonfire of registration certificates.

1909 In February, he is sentenced to three months' imprisonment in Volksrust and Pretoria jails. In November, he is arrested for third time.

1913 In September, leads two thousand Indian miners from New Castle across Transvaal border in a third *satyagraha* campaign.

1914 In July, he leaves South Africa for the last time and returns to India.

1918 In February, he leads a millworkers' strike at Ahmedabad. Millowners agree to arbitration after his three-day fast—his first fast in India. In March, he leads *satyagraha* for peasants in Kheda. In April, he organizes a nationwide strike against the Rowlatt Bills, which stated that those suspected of sedition could be imprisoned without trial, and becomes editor of English weekly *Young India* and Gujarati weekly *Navajivan*.

1920 In April, elected president of All India Home Rule League.

1921 Resolves to wear only a loincloth to propagate *khadi* (homespun cotton). Mass civil disobedience follows; thousands are jailed.

1922 Suspends mass disobedience because of violence at Chawri Chawra and undertakes five-day fast of penance at Bardoli. Arrested at Sabarmati on charge of sedition for articles in *Young India*. Sentenced to six years' imprisonment in Yeravada jail.

1924 Released from jail. Spends the next four years spreading the use of *khadi* and the removal of untouchability.

1929 Arrested for burning foreign cloth in Calcutta.

1930 Proposes January 26 as National Independence Day. Third all-India *satyagraha* campaign. Sets out on March 12 from Sabarmati with seventy-nine volunteers on historic Salt March, 241 miles to the sea at Dandi. On April 6, he breaks the Salt Law at Dandi by making salt from seawater. On May 4, he is arrested and imprisoned in Yeravada jail.

1931 On January 26, he is released unconditionally with thirty other leaders. In March, the Gandhi lrwin Pact, which stated that all political prisoners be released except those charged with acts of violence, is signed. In August, he sails from Bombay for the Second Round Table Conference in London.

1932 In January, he is arrested in Bombay with Sardar Patel and detained without trial at Yeravada prison. While still in prison on September 20, he begins "fast unto death" in protest of British action giving separate electorate to untouchables. He concludes the fast on September 26 after the British accept the Yeravada Pact, under which the idea of a separate electorate is dropped.

1933 Begins weekly publication of *Harijan* in place of *Young India.* In November, he begins a ten-month tour of India to end untouchability.

1934 Congress passes "Quit India" resolution—the final nationwide *satyagraha* campaign with Gandhi as the leader.

1942 Arrested on August 9 with other Congress leaders and Kasturba and imprisoned in Aga Khan Palace, near Poona.

1944 His wife, Kasturba, dies in detention at Aga Khan Palace on February 22 at the age of seventy-four. After Gandhi's health declines he is unconditionally released on May 6. This was his last imprisonment; he had spent 2,338 days in jail during his lifetime. In September, he participates in talks with Jinnah of Muslim League in Bombay on Hindu-Muslim amity.

1947 Tours Bihar in March to lessen Hindu-Muslim tensions. Begins conferences in New Delhi with Lord Mountbatten and Jinnah. In May, he opposes Congress's decision to accept division of country into India and Pakistan. On August 15, India is partitioned and granted independence. Gandhi fasts and prays to combat riots in Calcutta. In September he visits Delhi and neighboring areas to stop rioting and to visit camps of refugees.

1948 Gandhi undertakes a five-day fast on January 13 to bring about communal unity. Gandhi is assassinated on January 30 by a Hindu fanatic, Nathuram Godse, while holding a prayer meeting at Birla House, Delhi. His last words: *"He Ram, He Ram"* ("Oh God, Oh God").

BIBLIOGRAPHY

Gandhi, Arun, Gandhi, Sunanda, and Carol Lynn Yellin. *The Forgotten Woman: The Untold Story of Kasturba Gandhi, Wife of Mahatma Gandhi*. Ozark Mountain Publishers, 1997.

Gandhi, Mohandas K. *All Men Are Brothers: The Life and Thoughts of Mahatma Gandhi as Told in His Own Words*. Continuum Publishing Company, 1980.

———. *An Autobiography: The Story of My Experiments with Truth*. Dover, 1983. A twentieth-century classic. Gandhi's autobiography.

———. *Gandhi on Non-Violence: Selected Texts from Gandhi's Non-Violence in Peace and War.* New Directions Publishing Corporation, 1968.

———. *Hand-Spun Cloth*. Greenleaf Books, 1983.

———. *Hind Swaraj or Indian Home Rule*. Greenleaf Books, 1981.

———. *Satyagraha in South Africa*. Greenleaf Books, 1979.

———. *Vows and Observances*. Berkeley Hills Books, 1999.

Gandhi, Mohandas K., and Dennis Dalton (editor). *Mahatma Gandhi: Nonviolent Power in Action*. Columbia University Press, 1995.

———. *Selected Political Writings.* Hackett Publishing Company, 1996.

Gandhi, Mohandas K., and Louis Fischer (editor). *Essential Gandhi: An Anthology of His Writings on His Life, Work and Ideas*. Random House, 1983.

Gandhi, Mohandas K., Gandhi, Arun, and Michael Nagler. *Book of Prayers*. Berkeley Hills Books, 1999.

Gandhi, Mohandas, and Raghaven Iyer (editor). *The Essential Writings of Mahatma Gandhi*. Oxford University Press, 1993.

Mehta, Ved. *Mahatma Gandhi and His Apostles*. Yale University Press, 1983.

Payne, Robert. *Life and Death of Mahatma Gandhi*. William S. Konecky Associates, 1994.

ABOUT THE EDITOR AND PHOTOGRAPHS

All of the photographs in this book appear courtesy of the National Gandhi Museum in New Delhi, with the exception of the image on p.115 (opposite), taken during the filming of the 1982 movie Gandhi. *Producer-director Richard Attenborough (left) performs a respectful "pranam," the Indian equivalent of a handshake, for villagers to emulate as Ben Kingsley portrays Gandhi.*

To prepare for making his incredibly fine film about the life of Mahatma Gandhi, Attenborough studied Gandhi's own writings and speeches and all of the biographies written about him. Gandhi *was filmed almost entirely on location in India, and was released by Columbia Pictures.*

Richard Attenborough's international film and stage career as an actor, producer, and director spans sixty years. Among the films he has acted in are The Great Escape, The Sand Pebbles, *and Satyajit Ray's* The Chess Players. *He directed* Oh! What a Lovely War, Young Winston, A Bridge Too Far, A Chorus Line, Cry Freedom, *and* Shadowlands. Gandhi *received eight Academy Awards® in 1983, including Best Picture and Best Director. Attenborough was named Commander of the British Empire in 1967, was knighted in 1976 by Queen Elizabeth II, and was created a Life Peer in 1993, becoming Lord Attenborough. He is the author of* In Search of Gandhi. *Married with one son and two daughters, Attenborough lives in West London.*